PROGRESS
in
LITERATURE

T0345985

PROGRESS
IN LITERATURE

BY

LASCELLES ABERCROMBIE

*Professor of English Literature
in the University
of Leeds*

THE LESLIE STEPHEN LECTURE
DELIVERED AT CAMBRIDGE
10 MAY 1929

CAMBRIDGE
At the University Press
1929

CAMBRIDGE
UNIVERSITY PRESS

University Printing House, Cambridge CB2 8BS, United Kingdom

Published in the United States of America by Cambridge University Press, New York

Cambridge University Press is part of the University of Cambridge.

It furthers the University's mission by disseminating knowledge in the pursuit of education, learning and research at the highest international levels of excellence.

www.cambridge.org
Information on this title: www.cambridge.org/9781107634459

© Cambridge University Press 1929

First published 1929
Re-issued 2014

A catalogue record for this publication is available from the British Library

ISBN 978-1-107-63445-9 Paperback

PROGRESS IN LITERATURE

I WISH to put before you some reflections on *literary history*; and from this general topic to lead up to the problem which the title of my discourse indicates—the problem of *progress* in literature. Is there such a thing as progress in literature? If so, in what sense? What do we mean by 'progress' here? These are the questions which I shall try to answer; but I shall have to go over a good deal of ground before I get to them, in order to approach them at what seems to me the proper angle. My paper would have been more accurately called 'Progress in poetry'; since, in order to simplify the problem, and keep it within manageable dimensions, it is mainly to poetry that I shall refer. But I hesitated to employ—in Cambridge, especially—a title which might seem to verge too boldly on such a celebrated one as 'The Progress of Poesy'; the more so since I am not quite sure what 'progress,' in Gray's Pindaric sense, exactly means. But what I have to say about poetry will, if there is any truth in it, apply to literature at large. I begin, then, with some general considerations of literary history.

I

The systematic and scientific study of the history of literature, on the scale and with the importance which it has assumed nowadays, depending as it does on the plentiful accumulation and assured preservation of books (to say nothing of their multiplication), is one of the by-products of printing. Indeed, literary history is perhaps only a special case of by far the most notable result of that invention. For it would hardly be an exaggeration to say, that with the invention of printing, civilization at last acquired something like security of tenure. 'Hours in a Library' are not merely hours spent among the achievements of the past; they are hours spent in realizing how obstinately the past refuses to die, and insists on transforming itself into the present: provided, at least, the reader has in him anything like the intelligence of that fine spirit, in memory of whom I have the honour of lecturing to you to-day, and the library is anything like what Leslie Stephen would have thought worthy of being called one. Now civilization essentially depends on the ability of the past to continue into the life of the present; not merely as a mould or condition, but as an active energy. Once effectively break that continuity of past with present, and civilization, there and then, is at an end. Well, so long as books endure, that continuity is assured. The grand tyrant of ancient China knew where his enemy was vulnerable, when he wished to abolish the civilization that abhorred his rule; but, now that they are printed, the 'burning of the books' is no longer practical politics. It is thrilling to be told that civilization goes in cycles, or that a world-wide cataclysm is at hand; but a glance at our bookshelves may reassure us. There may be terrible things in store for the world; but, with literature in the position printing has put it in, it is hardly thinkable that civilization will ever again be *destroyed*, as it has been so often in the past.

It should seem, then, having regard to all this, that no study could be more deserving than literary history. But the devil's advocate is seldom at a loss: certainly not here. It is bad enough (I understand him to say) that *printed matter* should have usurped so vast a place in the life of the world to-day: that what our ancestors vividly took from life, we take, cut and dried, from books: that such a formidable, and such a steadily increasing, proportion of these books should actually be books about books. No nation ever had more reverence for literature than the ancient Chinese; yet, with the 'burning of the books' as one of the great disasters in their history, they declined to provide against its repetition by inventing printing, even though they had got as far as inventing moveable types. This need not surprise us. They invented gun-powder, but they declined to invent guns: they were content with fireworks. Can they have been governed by a similar prudence when, having invented moveable types, they refrained from inventing printing? Did their prophetic instinct warn them by some such vision as that in which John Davidson saw the future of Europe—a multitude of people, each balancing a lofty pile of books on his head, their gait oppressed and controlled by the weight of literature on their lives?

This kind of argument is, no doubt, too sweeping to be very effective; and does not really touch, though it may approach, the question of literary history. Moreover, the answer to it seems not very difficult. 'But,' the infernal advocate goes on, 'the answer to it must assume that those books on which printing confers immortality deserve their immortality. That, I say, would be bad enough in the long run: it scarcely lessens the horror of Davidson's vision of humanity in its book-ridden future. But the point is, that with the advent of literary history, it is no longer true that printed immortality is the reward of merit:

> the time has been
> That, when the brains were out, the man would die,
> And there an end;

and so with books. But now they do not die; literary history sees to that; the immortality of books is wholesale, indiscriminating, whether there are brains in them or not. "He that raises a Library," says William Wotton, in his *Reflections upon Ancient and Modern Learning*, "he that raises a Library, takes in Books of all Values; since bad Books have their Uses to Learned Men, as well as good ones." It is too true: very often the worst books give the clearest reflexion of tendencies, influences, fashions, conventions, movements, and other matters precious to the literary historian: it is the very absence of that confusing and unaccountable element, genius, that endears them to him. Look, for instance, at *The Castle of Otranto*. Candidly, would it be possible to find, on any bookstall to-day, trash sillier than this? But it is trash of the utmost importance in the history of English literature. No one can pretend to understand the growth of the romantic movement who has not studied this imbecility. It is a typical case. The flotsam of current literature is zealously preserved, the jetsam of the past anxiously rescued. Wotton supposes[1] that his remark would be as true of Alexandria as

[1] But he obviously misunderstands Temple's argument here.

of any modern library. If it were so, a kindly catastrophe set that right. But nowadays, with literature secured and perpetuated by the multiplying art of printing, not only our national libraries, desperately digging pits to contain the masses of typography entrusted to them, but all the reference libraries in every considerable town, are piously storing immortal rubbish for the benefit of those who study, or will study, literary history.'

The sting of this is in its tail. For certainly, considering the material that is being collected for it, the *future* of literary history, if it is to be carried on with the ideals of minute, impartial and intensive study which now inspire it, is not a comfortable thing to think of. But human nature has a knack of adjusting itself, and getting out of impossible situations; and it should always be possible to make the most voracious glutton exercise some principle of selection, by presenting him with a bill of fare sufficiently enormous. As things are at present, however, we may perhaps allow this much force to the reasoning of the devil's advocate: that if we are to understand the history of literature, a certain number of books must be read which would not be worth reading otherwise, and of which it may be said that only literary history keeps them alive. And suppose we do understand the history of literature: what is the good of that? Why, the good of it is just this: that without an understanding of literary history, no author can be properly appreciated—no author can give us all the enjoyment he is capable of giving. I do not mean that we are enabled to make excuses for shortcomings due to a writer's period and surroundings, or for out-of-date fashions and conventions. Such things, aesthetically speaking, can never be excused; though it is often decent to ignore them, and often interesting to account for them. But what I mean is just this: that the better we see an author's place in the history of literature, the better we see his merits as an individual artist.

This has been thought a paradox; and since this is, at bottom, the real reason for the existence of literary history, its denial has been urged against the very possibility of any such thing as literary history. But really it is no more of a paradox than to say that you get more out of the *Aeneid* if you know the *Georgics*, more out of the *Divine Comedy* if you know the *Vita Nuova*, more out of *Hamlet* if you know the *Midsummer Night's Dream*. Yet the objection has some weight, and is worth noticing. We may put it in this way. If a work of pure literature has any merit at all, the merit will be unique. Unless it can give us something we cannot get elsewhere, it will not count as literature; it certainly will not survive—except, perhaps, as an historical document to be studied, admittedly, in the interests of those works which *have* merit. But indeed, provided the author be competent and sincere, how can a work of art be anything else but unique? It can never occur again, unless the same experience could happen again to the same man at the same moment. But we need not consider the doctrine of eternal recurrence, any more than we need consider forgers and copyists. Now how can there be any continuity between things each one of which exists by being unique? And how can there be any history of things between which there is no continuity?

This is not a merely theoretical objection. That it does indicate a real difficulty, literary history itself too often shows—or rather, the failure of literary history to justify its name. For sometimes it deals with literature, but is not history; and sometimes it is history, but not of literature. To describe and criticize, in chronological order, a series of works of art is not to write history; and if the series of criticisms be merged in a series of biographies, with full accounts of ancestry, education, and so forth, even then it will not be history, unless very indirectly: that is to say, unless it can show how a man's art is the product of his life, and his life the product of his time and circumstance: both of which are enterprises requiring talents more than human. On the other hand, to write, however justly, the history of ideas and sentiments, of intellectual, social and political conditions, and of the way these are reflected in literature, is not to write the history of literature; for literature does not consist of these things, nor even of the way it reflects these things. Between these two modes of failure, a compromise is possible, which yields a third; and

this perhaps is the commonest in England—
something which is not quite history dealing
with something which is not quite literature.

No doubt a work may fail to be literary
history, and yet be invaluable as something
else. But surely it is as obvious as anything
can be that literature, simply and strictly as
literature, has a history of its own: I mean
that it exhibits a continuous process which
can be traced and expounded, without vio-
lating the principle that literary merit, like all
artistic merit, must always be unique. Let me
give you a simple instance of the way literature can present itself as a thing of which you
cannot ignore the history. Congreve was a
man of extraordinary ability; no one has ever
had a more exquisite sense of absurdity; and
underneath the brilliance of his wit, the rich-
ness of his humour, and the subtle nicety of
his style, there is always the solid ground of
common sense. That is, when he was writing
prose. But Congreve also cultivated, not
without satisfaction, the art of poetry. In the
'irregular ode,' *On Mrs Arabella Hunt Singing*,
Silence is first invoked, very properly, and

with all possible ceremony of phrase and
image:

Let all be husht, each softest Motion cease,
Be every loud tumultuous Thought at Peace,
    And every ruder Gasp of *Breath*
    Be calm, as in the *Arms* of Death.

After a good deal of this, 'Love-sick Maids
and wounded Swains' are invited, and told
to repress their groans, since, when Mrs Hunt
sings, 'a wondrous *Balm* between her Lips
she wears,' and this 'gentle Charmer' (by
which he means the Balm, not the lady who
wears it)

    to the tender Grief soft *Air* applies,
      Which, warbling Mystic Sounds,
    Cements the bleeding Panter's wounds.

At last, when the bleeding Panters have been
rendered unnoticeable, Silence is once more
invoked, in a phrase which somewhat boldly
identifies it with the other guests:

Hither let naught but sacred *Silence* come,
    And let all saucy Praise be dumb.

And now arrives the great moment—the
climax of poetic elaboration:

And lo! *Silence* himself is here;
Methinks I see the Midnight God appear;
  In all his downy Pomp array'd,
    Behold the rev'rend *Shade*:
An ancient Sigh he sits upon,
Whose Memory of Sound is long since gone,
And purposely annihilated for his Throne:
Beneath, two soft transparent Clouds do
    meet,
In which he seems to sink his softer Feet....
A Wreath of Darkness round his Head he
    wears,
Where curling Mists supply the Want of
    Hairs.

Immediately after this sublime image, there come, with somewhat startling effect, three very good lines:

But hark! the heav'nly Sphere turns round,
    And *Silence* now is drown'd
    In Extasy of Sound.

Unluckily, the heavenly Sphere suggests angels; and at once, from their 'lov'd Mansions in the Sky,' down comes 'all th' Immortal Throng':

See how they croud, see how the little
    Cherubs skip!
While others sit around her Mouth, and sip
Sweet Hallelujahs from her Lip.

Now, if we regard Congreve as an isolated phenomenon, this is simply inexplicable. The point is not merely that a writer of good prose should prove himself a very bad poet; but that *such* poetry—poetry of just this quality of badness—should have been seriously written by the author of *Love for Love* and *The Way of the World*—yes, and of *The Mourning Bride*. How came these absurdities to pass themselves off on the mind of Congreve, of all people?

But regard Congreve as an *historical* phenomenon, and all this becomes perfectly explicable. See him in his place in the process of literature; think of him as a person of indifferent poetic faculties, honestly doing his best to employ what, in accordance with the imperceptible pressure of his time, he instinctively understood to be the proper manner of poetry; and you might almost say, that to seat Silence upon an ancient Sigh is just the sort of poetic rapture you might expect to happen.

Or look at eighteenth-century poetry. How, if we have regard *solely* to the principle of unique achievement in poetry, can we account for the notorious fact that the style, say, of Addison, Pope, Savage, Johnson—all poets of distinctly individual character—can be instantly recognized as *belonging* to the eighteenth century? That, again, is a genuinely historical phenomenon; there we have the topic of literary history. For the fact is, that when we say a work of art is unique, we mean it in the sense in which we say a man is an individual. He is an individual, but in the midst of a society—or, to put it quite generally, in the midst of circumstances. Nay, he is an individual precisely because he is in the midst of circumstances. I do not mean anything so absurd as to say that his circumstances give him his individuality; but he would not be the individual he is without them; and indeed an individual person is not thinkable except as a being having relations with a world. Well, suppose this being has the experiences, and finds the words to express them, which entitle him to be called a poet. These experiences and these words exhibit him in his individual character; and precisely by doing so, exhibit also his circumstances, the relations between him and his world.

So that every poem will show us an aspect in which it is unique, as the utterance of a unique personality; and also an aspect in which it belongs to the process of events and tendencies its author lived in. We may say, perhaps, that it has both an aesthetic and an historical aspect.

The separation of these two aspects, however, is only notional, for the convenience of discussion. Indeed, when literary history really justifies itself, the two aspects re-unite; for, as I have already remarked, the more the historical aspect is understood, the more the aesthetic aspect can be enjoyed. Just as you will find more to enjoy in *Hamlet* if you know the rest of Shakespeare, so you will find more in Shakespeare if you know the Elizabethan drama. It is simply that neither an individuality nor the utterance of individuality can be fully appreciated *as such* if it is robbed of its birthright—the relationships which alone made it possible. Knowledge of a man's circumstances does not detract from, it reveals, his individuality. But in the case of a poet, the important circumstances are those which we may compendiously call literary.

Social, political and other conditions may have their significance, and need not be ignored. But it is with literary circumstances that literary history, as a specific science, must concern itself. It was not social or political or economic conditions that insinuated into Congreve's mind the poetic instinct to seat Silence upon an ancient Sigh, or into the minds of the eighteenth-century poets the instinct to write in the eighteenth-century manner.

Is then literary history simply the record of fluctuating fashions in literature, successions of influence, alternations of liberty and convention? These are very remarkable things, and literary history can hardly make too much of them. But if these were all its matter, it would, perhaps, scarcely deserve the name of *history*; it would be little better than literary *annals*. The circumstances men live in are a flux of continuous change. Every hour is the heir of the culture and tradition of the past, and the ancestor of the culture and tradition of the future. It is hardly necessary to prove that literature partakes of this movement of perpetual organic change. If it did not, it would be the only thing in the world that stands still. Those, at any rate, who have read some of our recent poetry will have realized the fact, if not the direction, of literature's power to move; but without such startling evidence, this should be sufficiently clear from any considerable survey of the chronology of letters. The law governing literary history must therefore be to discover and exhibit the nature and the continuity of this inevitable movement; or, as we may now call it, the principle of progress in literature. To do so, however, it is important to remember that literature is not merely a passenger in this world of change, carried onward by the combined movement of society, economics, politics, morals and manners. It has a distinct movement of its own; and it is the main business of literary history to trace the progress peculiar to literary art, however it may be entwined with the progress of all the other things. The contrast between life and literature may, no doubt, be very vicious and deceitful; but it may also be convenient, and in such a connexion as this is easily understood. Now nothing can be more fallacious than to equate the history of literature with the history of life: in an obvious example, to draw a picture of Restoration society from Restoration drama.[1] Life creates its traditions, and literature creates its traditions; they are profoundly and subtly related; but they are not the same tradition.

What then is the principle of progress in literature—the nature of that forward movement, that process of continual organic change, which is peculiar to literature, and which should, I say, be the chief concern of literary history? For without being governed by such a principle, it is difficult to see how that history can exist. But when I speak of a *forward movement*, it will not, I hope, be

[1] Professor G. M. Trevelyan has, I know, lately given us a striking story of Restoration life rivalling the plot of a Restoration play. But I think it is only because it does this that it seems characteristic of the time: it might have occurred at any time. Such sporadic instances do not give a picture of society; and it would be a queer puzzle (as Mr Edgar Stoll points out in reply) if we were to try to reconstruct life under Louis XIV from the plays of Corneille and Racine. See letters in the *Times Literary Supplement*, Jan. 5 and March 1, 1928.

supposed that I mean a process by which literature is continually getting better and better. Ignorance is often cheerful; but it would have to be a very cheerful ignorance to support such an optimism as that. Yet the advance of literature towards perfection has been proclaimed several times; though it would not be easy to say what perfection here can mean; nor is it necessary for the word progress to mean anything more than the capacity for change implicit in the nature of a thing becoming gradually explicit in its continual adjustment to circumstance. The notion, it is true, that literature is *improving*, has usually been based on a short view of things: but that has not prevented it from being very positively asserted; as it has been, in fact, to-day. For everyone has heard how literature, since the Victorians, has *progressed* —in the perfectionist sense. But one of the lesser services of literary history, is to rate these vagaries of criticism at their proper value. In the eighteenth century, people thought that poetry had advanced decidedly nearer to perfection than in the Elizabethan age; and the Romantics were quite sure their poetry was a marvellous improvement on the despised tradition of the eighteenth century. To us, the notion that the Elizabethans were barbarians, or that the poets of the eighteenth century were contemptible, seems merely amusing; and just as amusing some day, we may be sure, will be the current opinion of the Victorians. But these feelings of superiority over a previous age are not difficult to explain. Change in the tradition of literary art does not maintain a uniform pace, or anything like it; and sometimes seems to go so fast that it feels like a revolution—at any rate, like a revolt. Passions are engendered, which form a sort of patriotism of the moment; and what more natural for the partakers in the revolution than to despise the regime it seems to have overthrown, and to believe that poetry has thereby taken a step forward towards perfection? Political revolutions inspire similar dreams.

But leaving aside henceforth all ideas of *improvement*, I go on now to suggest an answer to our question, What is the principle of progress in literature? Two things must be said as preface to this attempt. First, the principle can only be a very general one; otherwise it could not possibly include the immense variety of the ways in which literature has changed, developed, grown, and gone in this direction and that. Remember too that I am only considering the historic aspect, not at all the aesthetic aspect, of literature; I am not proposing to account for genius, or whatever it may be that can give to a work of literary art the merit which is unique. Neither am I concerned with the influence of genius; nor with casual fashion, imitation, the invasion of foreign influence, change directly caused by changes in the things by which literature is surrounded. The principle of literary progress, of the movement peculiar to literature as it exists in its own right, must be such that it will allow for the operation of these things: once more, it must be a very general principle. But in the second place, the principle must be of such a kind that it can be associated and harmonized with the processes of change in the rest of life.

II

It might seem advisable to approach our question through comparison with the other arts. But that would not help us much, for the problem is the same in all, and in all presents the same initial difficulty—the familiar difficulty of matter and manner: since all art consists of expressive communication by means of a symbolical technique. To make the principle of progress refer to the matter of an art would satisfy no one; neither would anyone be satisfied if it referred to the manner. It could only be satisfactory if it referred, equally and at once, to both. But unfortunately it seems impossible to examine any art precisely without making this separation of meaning and medium. The sort of approach we want is one which will put us in such a position, that whatever is said of either matter or manner will of necessity involve the other; so that the distinction will be harmless. Such an approach, I think, may be made by a comparison, or contrast, of poetry and philosophy.

Poetry has this in common with philosophy: both depend on language, yet both seek to transcend the ordinary habits of language. And for the same reason; for both poetry and philosophy endeavour, by means of language, to represent *reality*: which is not the usual concern of language. But each finds a different defect in language, and tries to improve it in a different direction. The language of ordinary life is too rigid for the poet; for the philosopher, it is not rigid enough. The poet requires, besides every variety of meaning which ordinary language can give him, a vast of meaning which ordinary language cannot possibly give him. The philosopher wishes to confine language solely to a strict exactitude of logical meaning; and ordinary language is for ever disturbing his logic by irrelevant insinuations of other sorts of meaning. Now for philosophy, pursuing its reality further and further into the utmost purity of intellectual abstraction, the difficulty has, it seems, been growing more and more acute: as anyone may see in a glance —and for most people a glance would be enough—at the pages of those philosophers who, following the lead of George Boole, have endeavoured to construct by mathematical artifices a *perfect language* of universal and inflexible exactitude. And even that has not disposed of the difficulty. It appears that philosophy nowadays feels bound to suspect not merely this or that language, but any conceivable language at all; so that finally we are seriously warned 'that nothing correct can be *said* in philosophy.' Since it is philosophy itself that says this, it might seem that, having thus landed itself in the celebrated position of the Cretan liar, there is nothing to be done but to leave it there. But in fact the position is extraordinarily interesting, and not without some bearing on our question. You will most conveniently find it explained in Mr Bertrand Russell's introduction to Wittgenstein's *Tractatus Logico-Philosophicus*, from which I just now quoted that remarkable warning, and which is, whether it really introduces Wittgenstein or not, a wonderfully keen and most exciting piece of reasoning. In summary form, the position is this. If, in philosophy, language represents reality, it only does so by its structure; and no language can *say* what its structure *shows*: it cannot put its own structure into words, it can only repeat its structure. That is to say, the philosophical expressiveness of any language is itself, in that language, inexpressible. In other words, the language of philosophy cannot *say* what it *means*. Its representation of reality could only be disengaged by constructing a higher language, which would stand to the first as the first stands to the world. And having done that, a third would have to be constructed to represent the meaning of the second; and so it would have to go on, until you might have, as Mr Russell suggests, an endless hierarchy of languages.

It is an inspiring vision; but there is, to me, an element of desperation in it. Look now at the way poetry solves its opposite problem: for poetry, too, finds itself compelled to construct a higher language. It is not here, however, that we must look for progress: poetry *begins* by solving its problem, its existence consists in the solution. And the solution is found, not in a hierarchy of languages, but in one extremely complex technique which, though made out of ordinary language, amounts to a triumphantly effective *superlanguage*—what we call poetic diction. By means of this, poetry can not only represent its reality; poetic diction, besides *meaning* reality, can also *say* what it means.

But, philosophy might here object, this claim to represent reality is not after all so very remarkable; for we all know that in the matter of reality, poetry is easily satisfied. Quite true, retorts poetry; I am easily satisfied because I know what I mean by reality, which is more than anyone dare say about philosophy.—As for me, I am not called on to take sides in this dispute; but I confess, that whenever I read that great passage in Lucretius declaring how impossible it is that the senses should ever be deceived, something within me will not be restrained by my consciousness of its presumption from whispering, 'There, just there, is where philosophy has gone wrong!' For how can the senses be deceived? To say the eyes are deceived is to say they do not see what they do see; and if sight and reason disagree, why must it be reason that gives us the reality, and sight the delusion? Is it, perhaps, because, since

Epicurus, philosophy has sinned against the senses, allowing reason to discredit them, and considering reality as an intellectual abstraction from life, that what Dante calls the eternal grief of the philosophers has descended in retribution on their schools? At any rate, it has never occurred to poetry to discredit the senses; and the eternal grief of the philosophers—their vision of a final reality perpetually eluding them—is unknown to poetry. For in the senses, poetry possesses reality, without incurring the corresponding absurdity of discrediting intellect. Reality, for poetry, consists in nothing more, but in nothing less, than *being alive*: in poetry, sense, intellect, and spirit all equally give reality. In a word, reality, for poetry, is *experience*. Even if poetry expresses man's struggle to capture the unknown, it is the *struggle* that poetry expresses—delighting in the experience of intellectual tragedy even as in the experience of delicious sensation.

The reality of experience, then, is what poetry has to represent; and it does so by what we call poetic diction—an unusual elaboration, over the common syntax of language, of the power of suggestion in words, and of both the rhythms and the syllabic qualities of their sound. The combination has an extraordinary range and variety of expressiveness; and though its representation, however precise and just, may perhaps never be theoretically complete, it can nevertheless be practically adequate to the infinite range and endless variety of experience. Moreover, this poetic diction, unlike the language of philosophy, does not merely represent by an inexpressible structure: it can say what it means. Poetry, unlike philosophy, does not give us a copy or picture or projection of its reality: it represents reality by actually and truly calling reality into existence: it creates reality over again. For to say that poetry represents experience, is to suppose that a person is reading a poem; and as he reads, the poet's experience once more *lives* in the mind of the reader. To effect this, the poet required a higher language, simply because ordinary language is not adapted to his purpose. But having once found the right kind of higher language—the technique of poetic diction—

that suffices him. He has no need of a hierarchy of superlanguages in order to disengage his meaning; for his meaning disengages itself: it instantly comes to life as the thing itself whenever his technique operates. His meaning, in a word, is creative.

Thus it makes no difference now whether we talk about matter or manner, poetic diction or poetic experience, the reality or its representation; for whatever is said about the one will necessarily involve the other. If we think of the matter of poetry, it is easy to see how every poem, though it must be a unique phenomenon, must nevertheless belong to history; since precisely that is true of experience. And truly to know an experience, and feel all there is in it, we must know it on both sides; and that is what happens when a poem means to us not only itself, but its place in history. But as regards progress, we are more likely to get a hint of the principle we are looking for, if we consider the technique of poetry. The medium of poetry is not, strictly speaking, language, but that unusual elaboration of language which we call poetic diction. This, of course, is not the whole of poetic technique; there is besides that immensely important part of it which we call poetic form. Still, it seems not unreasonable, in this matter of progress, to expect some analogy between poetic technique and the raw material of its medium—common speech. For, after all, poetic diction is no more than the deliberate cultivation and effective management of forces, the rudiments of which common speech casually and ineffectively betrays; and poetic form has itself some analogy with syntax.

Now if there is one thing in the world that shows progress—the continuous movement of organic change—it is language. The nature of this movement is well known; it is what philologists call the change from synthesis to analysis. It may take several forms; but it will be sufficient for our purpose if I give you the stock example. Where Latin says *fuissem*, English says *I should have been*: the complex of ideas which Latin synthesizes into a single word, English analyzes into four words. The difference between Latin and English which this example indicates gives us the general law of linguistic progress; it is thus that

Latin developed into Italian, Anglo-Saxon into English. The process is not, of course, uniform; some languages, such as English and Chinese, have gone further in analysis than others, such as German. And in any case, synthetic and analytic are comparative terms: Latin is synthetic compared with English, but analytic compared with some savage tongues. There could not be an absolutely synthetic language: there will never be an absolutely analytic language. But the change from synthesis to analysis is the great law governing the history of language. We are most familiar with it in the replacement of inflexion and concord by auxiliary words and the enhanced importance of word-order. But it may take many forms; and in one form or another it seems to be universal. This is surely what we might expect; since it corresponds with what we may well suppose to be the movement of consciousness itself—the movement by which, broadly speaking, man has continually become, not indeed *more* conscious of his world, but more *analytically* conscious of it. For our consciousness of the world comes to us in masses; it is only by analytical attention that we split it up into component parts. By the interplay of language and consciousness, the habit of analysis seems to have been growing on man throughout his history; so that the difference between Homer's world and ours has some correspondence with the difference between Greek and English. We are surprised at the complex grammar and enormous vocabulary of some primitive tongues. Thus, instead of our system of pronouns, we find savages using single words for such ideas as 'you here,' 'you there,' 'he sitting down,' 'he standing up,' and so on. Clearly, the savage's vocabulary names his consciousness of things in large, unanalyzed masses; and the seeming paradox follows, that complexity of structure in a language results from the simplicity of unanalyzing habits of consciousness, whereas the simplicity of modern analytical grammar directly answers to our immeasurably more complex consciousness of the world. And the tendency to analysis in language not only allows room for consciousness to complicate itself, in accordance with what seems to be its destiny; it allows consciousness to discriminate its component parts, and put whatever emphasis it likes on any one of them.

Now I suggest that the principle of progress in the art of literature is exactly analogous with the principle of progress in language: it is that kind of change which, if we measure it over a sufficient interval, presents itself as the change from synthesis to analysis. It is very gradual, often so slow as to be hardly noticeable; it is not a uniform movement, either as regards time or place; it is often at the mercy of other kinds of movement. But it is, I suggest, the one process which, whatever else may be happening in literature, is always there, always persists. Naturally, however, it will present itself in many ways, since the technique of literature includes all the modes both of diction and of form; but, if I am right, these modes of technique will correspond with modes of consciousness, of experience, which are *comparatively* synthetic or analytic.

Thus, when the poets of antiquity are said to be unaware of our modern sentiment for nature, it is nothing more than an analytical habit of thought comparing itself with a synthetic habit. Who can read the ancient poets, and believe them to be indifferent to nature? The thing simply is, that they do not analyze their feeling into explicit emphasis. The sea lives in Homer as nowhere else in poetry; but he never *says* that it lives, except in the characteristically synthetic way of deifying it. Virgil, in the *Aeneid*, seems haunted by the contrast between human life and the strange and lovely life of birds; but he does not bring the contrast out—still less does he work it out, as, for example, Leopardi does. So too, more generally, if landscape in ancient poetry seems to lack colour, that does not mean that the poets could not see colour distinctly; for them the colour of a natural object, and the function of the colour in their aesthetic experience, would be sufficiently implied by merely mentioning the object. A similar case of synthetic *texture* in poetry may be found in the epic use of 'stock epithets'; which is again a thing the analytical habit of mind does not easily appreciate. No doubt the stock epithet is a convention, but with Homer, that master of synthetic art, it may nevertheless imply a great deal of meaning peculiarly appropriate to the moment. Thus, throughout the seventh book of the *Odyssey*, in spite of Nausikaa and the kindly Phaeacians, it is a 'much-enduring' Odysseus that is impressed on us; and when, at the end of the book, night falls, it is still a 'much-enduring' man who goes to sleep— at last, after so many years, in a civilized bed again. The epithet is just. He is safe for the time; but he is worn out, uncertain of his fate, his sufferings still vivid in his mind (he has just been compelled to recall them). But when with the coming of dawn in the opening of the eighth book, Odysseus awakes, all this is changed. It is not the 'much-enduring' Odysseus, it is Odysseus the 'sacker of cities' that springs from his bed. Again a conventional epithet; but does not the force of it leap out at us here? The magic of sleep has done its work; the whole complexion of things is altered, he feels his fortunes have taken a turn—he feels himself, not now the 'much-enduring,' but once more the 'sacker of cities.' A psychological change which analytical art would delight to explore and emphasize, Homer represents by the change from one stock epithet to another. Such implicit meaning is not altogether unlike the meaning implicit in inflexion. And this is nothing exceptional. When Nausikaa is playing at ball with her maidens, she is the 'white-armed' Nausikaa: the stock epithet is, for Homer, a sufficient picture of the gestures of the game: in that context, the whole picture is implicit in the single word. When Ares tells Aphrodite that their opportunity has come, 'for Hephaistos has gone to visit the savage-speaking Sintians,' the epithet is no doubt the right one for those barbarians; but how deliciously right it is also in the mouth of Ares at just this moment! How perfectly that one word ἀγριοφώνους contains his scorn for Hephaistos—cultivating the worship of those gabblers! The adulterer's contempt for the husband: one word suffices to *imply* it.

These instances all come close together in the *Odyssey*. I have taken them almost at random; but a surprisingly long list could be made of cases in which stock epithets, far from being merely conventional, synthesize very complex meanings. Indeed, the mere existence of stock epithets seems to me a sign of synthetic art. And those master-strokes of what is sometimes called Homeric restraint —as in Nausikaa's farewell, or in the comment of the old men when they catch sight of Helen on the walls—'No wonder the young men suffer for her!'—these too seem to belong to that stage of art in which meaning is synthesized rather than analyzed: which must not be taken to suggest anything like a crude or uncultivated stage of art. It would be difficult to misunderstand poetry more grossly, than to apply such terms to the exquisite polish and studied accomplishment of Homer.

But, since poetic form is further from the direct influence of language than poetic texture or diction, an analogy *there*, if we could find one, between linguistic and aesthetic progress, would be much more striking; and thus more likely to convince us that art progresses by moving from synthesis to analysis. We do not have to look very far for such an analogy. Think of the form of Attic drama, and the form of Elizabethan drama: is not the difference exactly paralleled by the difference between *fuissem* and *I should have been*—or rather by the difference between the compact interlocked meaning of a *sentence* synthesized by concord and inflexion, and the meaning which is analyzed into separable parts by auxiliary words only held together by their proper order? The dramatic syntax of Shakespeare and of Sophokles both equally arrive at a final unity. But in Sophokles, the whole dictates its nature to the parts, in Shakespeare the parts consent to make a whole; in Sophokles, the interest of the shapely whole manifestly presides over the detail from start to finish, in Shakespeare an elaborate emphasis of the detail is compatible with the organization of the whole. But if the difference between the structure of ancient Greek and of modern English indicates a progressive change from synthetic to analytic consciousness of things, is it not just what we should expect, that a similar difference, given a large enough interval, should reveal itself also in the form, and not merely in the texture, of the art of literature?

We must not, however, as I have said, expect a constant and uniform movement in art, any more than in language: here it will go quickly, there it will lag. I suspect that the regular epic form belongs distinctly to that stage of art which is synthetic rather than analytic—terms which, remember, are only used in comparison against each other. For epic is not merely narrative, not merely heroic narrative—a tale of heroic acts and manners. It is heroic narrative in which is implicit some version of the destiny of man, some symbolism of an attitude of faith or understanding in the world: a meaning which must always be more than can be explicitly said, but which the whole action of the poem is designed to make us profoundly feel. This is just the form of art which the synthetic habit of mind would invent and use; but it has been carried on into modern times not only by the passion of Tasso and the majesty of Milton, but even into our own day in that monumental performance, *The Dawn in Britain*. It is notable, however, that Doughty, whose character seems a survival from some earlier age, had an instinctive abhorrence of all analytical habits of thought. He scarcely succeeded in his attempt to put the English language back again into synthetic structure; but the splendour of *Adam Cast Forth* shows that both in art and in thought, especially religious thought, it is still possible for genius to be grandly unanalyzing. In fact, he was just the man in whom the epic tradition might come to life again once more.

Those critics, however, are probably right, who regard the regular epic as an exception to, rather than as according with, the tendency of the modern world: an opinion which is sometimes crudely and rather foolishly expressed by calling the modern epics 'artificial.' We may, at any rate, regard the survival of the regular epic into modern times as an instance of what a physicist might call a *lag* in the rate of progress from synthesis to analysis. And it must be admitted that there is sometimes a certain difficulty apparent in the work of synthesizing modern thoughts and feelings into epic form. Tasso does not quite succeed in combining human and supernatural affairs; in Camoëns the synthesis is often simply unreasonable. The difficulty may even be alleged, without blasphemy, against Milton himself. Those who criticize God the Father in *Paradise Lost* sometimes forget that he figures there as a person in a story, who must therefore have a delineated character: and that can only be in the likeness of humanity. Milton does this to admiration; and yet the symbolic delineation seems somehow incomplete. Some of the material which should have gone to compose the figure of deity seems to have slipped through the poet's fingers. When he wrote *Paradise Lost*, Milton had arrived at a most subtle and profound religious philosophy; the whole poem is instinct with it, and it is certainly present in God the Father's superb self-vindications. Yet his figure is not quite adequate to the place and function of deity in Milton's vast conception of things— a conception almost as difficult to seize as Spinoza's. We may suppose (since it is Milton who fails) that it was not humanly possible to reduce such matter to the epic form.

But something similar is to be found much earlier than this in the history of epic. Virgil is one of the most interesting poets in the world because he seems to belong to two worlds. In him the ancient tradition continues, and the modern consciousness begins. 'Sunt lacrymae rerum': who has not felt that poignant phrase? But it is not easy to be quite sure what it means. And perhaps the Virgilian pregnancy may sometimes be due to an imperfect sympathy between old tradition and some subtle novelty of feeling. It is never a discord; his marvellous art makes that impossible. But he does seem sometimes to compact into synthetic form sensibilities which are striving towards analysis. That, at any rate, could not be said of any of his predecessors. A very gradual, but perceptible, process towards analysis could be traced in Greek poetry, which might be baldly indicated by the names of Homer, Sophokles, and Theokritos. But when Virgil took over bucolic poetry from Theokritos, he gave it a spirit unlike anything that had been before; and as we look back on it, the change seems to have been decisive for the future of poetry. With Virgil it reaches its height in the *Aeneid*, and *there* in the character of Aeneas: one of the noblest pieces of psychological imagination in literature. Why has the character of

Aeneas been so often despised? By the weaker sort of critics, because, deceived by the poetic tradition, they have looked for something like Achilles, when they should have been looking for something like Hamlet. But by other critics, perhaps, because of the way such a character as Aeneas, and therefore such situations as events form round him, are presented to us. Thus, when Aeneas, after Dido's passionate entreaty and imprecation, finally rejects her and turns away to do his duty, the whole essence of the tragically complex situation is compressed by Virgil into the famous phrase, 'At pius Aeneas': the significant stock epithet once more! But Virgil is perhaps demanding more of synthetic art than it can decently be expected to give; and in consequence none of the great moments of poetry has been so egregiously misunderstood. For Aeneas' rejection of Dido, and sorrowful resumption of his god-given task, *is* one of the great moments of poetry; the more so, of course, because Dido is herself such a superb creature. But Aeneas is perfectly right, except for those shallow heads who believe in 'all for love, or the world well lost.' Virgil's art, however, is content to make both his hero's justification, and his agonized conquest of himself, implicit in the tremendous, untranslatable force of the one word *pius*; and perhaps it may be said that throughout the *Aeneid* there are occasions when Virgil demands so much of the art which he glorified anew, that he makes inevitable the coming of a greater freedom of analysis.

And thus Virgil, in this sense too, is Dante's guide. For with Dante, the progress of literature has arrived at such a stage that the whole art of poetry has become, in comparison with the poetry of antiquity, as distinctively analytic as Italian is in comparison with Latin. Dante's world is organized out of the myriad details, each one vivid with the utmost intensity of its peculiar nature, which his miraculous analysis distinguishes. But it is not only in Dante's texture that the epic intention frees itself from ancient tradition, and accommodates itself to the modern consciousness of things; it does so even more remarkably in his architecture. The series of incidents, each one apparently complete in itself, organizes itself into the grand tripartite unity of the order of divine justice; and though each may seem to make a separable impression on us, the design is absolute by which each contributes essentially to Hell, Purgatory, or Heaven; and Hell, Purgatory and Heaven themselves compose a single sublime whole. This is a structure as analytic in comparison with ancient regular epic (or its modern survivors) as Shakespeare's structure is in comparison with Sophokles'.

Dante's architecture, however, so entirely peculiar to his theme, could scarcely be repeated. But even if it be true that regular epic form is nowadays something of an anachronism—the word is perhaps a little too harsh— even if that be true, it does not follow that the epic intention cannot continue; and the modern consciousness of the world is as likely to need the great symbolic poem as the ancient. Modern literature, however, has invented a species of form which is entirely adequate to the epic intention, and can give its expression the fullest possible scope for analysis—the so-called dramatic poem. Just because of the opportunity it offers of organizing the full freedom of poetic analysis into clear poetic unity, the form of Elizabethan drama became the property not merely of the stage, but of literature in general. The variety of its possibility may be sufficiently suggested by mentioning Ibsen's *Brand* and Browning's *Pippa Passes*; and it is, in fact, the form adopted by the epic intention in two of the greatest symbolic poems of recent times— Goethe's *Faust* and Hardy's *The Dynasts*. In the latter of these two especially we may note the progress of poetry in the direction of analysis. In no other great symbolic poem has the significance been brought out into anything like the elaborate explicitness which Hardy achieved by his vastly expanded use of the form of analytical drama.

I could only, on such an occasion as this, indicate, in a few rather random instances, first, what I mean by synthesis and analysis in literary art, and secondly, the sort of grounds on which the principle of progress in literature which I suggest might be maintained. Remember, I do not pretend that principle to be anything but a very general one, nor that its operation is always uniform and manifest. But that man's consciousness of the world shows a gradual tendency towards analysis will hardly, I think, be disputed; and it is reasonable to suppose that the art of literature, one of the main engines of consciousness, should partake of that movement. The chief question for literary history will always be the manner in which literature partakes of the universal movement. I have mentioned some examples of this; but sometimes it may be no more than a choice of themes, or an emphasis on themes, which would hardly have been made at an earlier stage of the progress towards analysis. Thus, some of Hardy's lyrics express, in their strangely successful mixture of traditional and revolutionary technique, shades of feeling, thought, sensation, which are not only new to poetry, but which seem never to have been precisely distinguished before. That for a similar effect a revolutionary technique is not necessary, that it can be achieved in a new perfection of the classic style, let that great poet remind us, whom Cambridge, true to its long tradition of hospitality to the genius of English poetry, shelters to-day:

> To think that two and two are four
>   And neither five nor three
> The heart of man has long been sore
>   And long 'tis like to be.

With exquisite distinction, as so often in Mr Housman's work, a sentiment which must always have been implicit in man's mind becomes explicit in a manner peculiarly suited to the consciousness of to-day.

Remember, too, that this principle of progress which I allege carries with it no suggestion of improvement. As in language, so in art: in the progress from synthesis to analysis, something is lost in order that something else may be gained. But who shall strike the balance? If we have lost the secure dignity of the antique, we have gained variety and freedom of enterprise which antiquity could never know. It is best to regard the change as, simply, inevitable.